EASY BREAKF

COOKBOOK

DELICIOUS BREAKFAST RECIPES FOR OATMEAL, WAFFLES, AND EGGS

By
Chef Maggie Chow
Copyright © 2015 by Saxonberg Associates

Published by
BookSumo, a division of Saxonberg Associates
http://www.booksumo.com/

INTRODUCTION

Welcome to *The Effortless Chef Series*! Thank you for taking the time to download the *Easy Breakfast Cookbook*. Come take a journey with me into the delights of easy cooking. The point of this cookbook and all my cookbooks is to exemplify the effortless nature of cooking simply.

In this book we focus on Breakfast. You will find that even though the recipes are simple, the taste of the dishes is quite amazing.

So will you join me in an adventure of simple cooking? If the answer is yes (and I hope it is) please consult the table of contents to find the dishes you are most interested in. Once you are ready jump right in and start cooking.

— Chef Maggie Chow

TABLE OF CONTENTS

ANY ISSUES? CONTACT ME

If you find that something important to you is missing from this book please contact me at maggie@booksumo.com.

I will try my best to re-publish a revised copy taking your feedback into consideration and let you know when the book has been revised with you in mind.

:)

— Chef Maggie Chow

Legal Notes

Common Abbreviations

cup(s)	C.
tablespoon	tbsp
teaspoon	tsp
ounce	oz.
pound	lb

*All units used are standard American measurements

CHAPTER 1: OATMEAL RECIPES

CROCK POT OATMEAL I

Ingredients

- 1 C. steel cut oats
- 3 1/2 C. water
- 1 C. peeled and chopped apple
- 1/2 C. raisins
- 2 tbsps butter
- 1 tbsp ground cinnamon
- 2 tbsps brown sugar
- 1 tsp vanilla extract

Directions

- For 7 hours on low cook the following in your crock pot: vanilla extract, oats, brown sugar, water, cinnamon, apples, butter, and raisins.
- Enjoy with milk.

Amount per serving (6 total)

Timing Information:

Preparation	Cooking	Total Time
15 m	6 h	6 h 15 m

Nutritional Information:

Calories	208 kcal
Fat	5.6 g
Carbohydrates	37.2g
Protein	3.9 g
Cholesterol	10 mg
Sodium	35 mg

* Percent Daily Values are based on a 2,000 calorie diet.

CRANBERRY MAPLE OATMEAL

Ingredients

- 3 1/2 C. plain or vanilla soy milk
- 1/4 tsp salt
- 2 C. rolled oats
- 1/4 C. pure maple syrup
- 1/3 C. raisins
- 1/3 C. dried cranberries
- 1/3 C. sweetened flaked coconut
- 1/3 C. chopped walnuts
- 1 (8 oz.) container plain yogurt (optional)
- 3 tbsps honey (optional)

Directions

- Boil your milk in a large pan. Then combine in cranberries, oats, raisins, and maple syrup.
- Let this cook, boiling, for 6 mins. Then shut off the heat and add in your coconuts and walnuts.
- Before eating add a dollop of honey and yogurt.
- Enjoy.

Amount per serving (6 total)

Timing Information:

Preparation	Cooking	Total Time
5 m	10 m	15 m

Nutritional Information:

Calories	379 kcal
Fat	10.4 g
Carbohydrates	63.1g
Protein	11.6 g
Cholesterol	2 mg
Sodium	212 mg

* Percent Daily Values are based on a 2,000 calorie diet.

ROLLED OATS I

Ingredients

- 1 egg, beaten
- 1 3/4 C. milk
- 1/2 C. packed brown sugar
- 1 C. rolled oats
- 2 tbsps butter

Directions

- Get a big pot and pour in your milk then add: brown sugar and beaten eggs.
- Get everything boiling and continually stir the mix for about 4 mins.
- Shut off the heat and then add your butter.
- Let the butter melt.
- Enjoy warm.

Amount per serving (3 total)

Timing Information:

Preparation	Cooking	Total Time
5 m	10 m	15 m

Nutritional Information:

Calories	357 kcal
Fat	13.9 g
Carbohydrates	48.8g
Protein	10.5 g
Cholesterol	94 mg
Sodium	145 mg

* Percent Daily Values are based on a 2,000 calorie diet.

Oven Oatmeal I

Ingredients

- 3 C. rolled oats
- 1 C. brown sugar
- 2 tsps ground cinnamon
- 2 tsps baking powder
- 1 tsp salt
- 1 C. milk
- 2 eggs
- 1/2 C. melted butter
- 2 tsps vanilla extract
- 3/4 C. dried cranberries

Directions

- Set your oven to 350 degrees before doing anything else.
- Get a bowl, and mix: salt, melted butter, oats, cranberries, milk, baking powder, beaten eggs, cinnamon, vanilla extract, and brown sugar.
- Pour the mixture into a casserole dish coated with non-stick spray and cook in the oven for 45 mins.
- Enjoy warm.

Amount per serving (8 total)

Timing Information:

Preparation	Cooking	Total Time
10 m	40 m	50 m

Nutritional Information:

Calories	393 kcal
Fat	15.3 g
Carbohydrates	59.2g
Protein	6.8 g
Cholesterol	79 mg
Sodium	502 mg

* Percent Daily Values are based on a 2,000 calorie diet.

ROLLED OATS AND WHEAT GERM

Ingredients

- 1/2 C. rolled oats
- 1 C. water
- 1 tbsp honey
- 1 tbsp wheat germ
- 1 tsp flaxseed oil
- 1/4 C. soy milk

Directions

- For 6 mins microwave your oats and water.
- Then add in your flax oil, wheat germ, and honey.
- Finally add your milk and enjoy warm.

Amount per serving (1 total)

Timing Information:

Preparation	Cooking	Total Time
2 m	5 m	7 m

Nutritional Information:

Calories	318 kcal
Fat	9.2 g
Carbohydrates	52.2g
Protein	9 g
Cholesterol	0 mg
Sodium	35 mg

* Percent Daily Values are based on a 2,000 calorie diet.

HALLOWEEN OATS

Ingredients

- 1/2 C. old-fashioned rolled oats
- 1 C. soy milk
- 1/4 C. canned pumpkin puree
- 3 dashes ground cinnamon
- 1 tbsp chopped walnuts
- 1/2 tsp avocado honey

Directions

- Add the following to a big pot: cinnamon, oats, puree, and soy milk.
- Get everything boiling then lower the heat and let the mixture lightly boil for 7 mins. Add in your honey and oats, and let the oatmeal sit for 2 mins.
- Enjoy.

Amount per serving (1 total)

Timing Information:

Preparation	Cooking	Total Time
5 m	10 m	15 m

Nutritional Information:

Calories	244 kcal
Fat	9.7 g
Carbohydrates	31g
Protein	10.9 g
Cholesterol	0 mg
Sodium	273 mg

* Percent Daily Values are based on a 2,000 calorie diet.

HONEY WALNUT OATS

Ingredients

- 1/4 C. quick cooking oats
- 1/2 C. skim milk
- 1 tsp flax seeds
- 2 tbsps chopped walnuts
- 3 tbsps honey
- 1 banana, peeled

Directions

- For 3 mins microwave: banana, oats, honey, milk, walnuts, and flax. Stir the contents before serving in bowls.
- Enjoy.

Amount per serving (1 total)

Timing Information:

Preparation	Cooking	Total Time
5 m	2 m	7 m

Nutritional Information:

Calories	532 kcal
Fat	13.1 g
Carbohydrates	101.7g
Protein	11.2 g
Cholesterol	2 mg
Sodium	58 mg

* Percent Daily Values are based on a 2,000 calorie diet.

Cinnamon Ginger Carrot Oats

Ingredients

- 4 C. water
- 1 C. steel-cut oats
- 1 apple - peeled, cored, and chopped
- 1/2 C. shredded carrot
- 1/2 C. raisins
- 1 tsp ground cinnamon
- 1/2 tsp ground nutmeg
- 1/2 tsp ground ginger
- 1 pinch salt
- 1 tbsp butter
- 3/4 C. chopped pecans
- 1 tbsp brown sugar
- 1/2 C. plain yogurt

Directions

- Start by adding water to a big pot. Then get the water boiling.
- Once boiling add in your oats. Lower the heat and let the oats simmer for 12 mins.
- Then combine in: salt, apples, nutmeg, carrots, ginger, cinnamon, and raisins.
- Continue simmering the contents for another 19 mins.
- Get a frying pan and fry your pecans in butter for 4 mins.
- Top the pecans with brown sugar continue to cook for 2 more mins.
- Before eating your oatmeal, add some pecan mix and a tbsp of yogurt.
- Enjoy.

Amount per serving (6 total)

Timing Information:

Preparation	Cooking	Total Time
15 m	40 m	55 m

Nutritional Information:

Calories	287 kcal
Fat	13.9 g
Carbohydrates	37.7g
Protein	6.2 g
Cholesterol	6 mg
Sodium	41 mg

* Percent Daily Values are based on a 2,000 calorie diet.

WET OATS

Ingredients

- 3 3/4 C. water
- 2 C. rolled oats
- 1 pinch salt
- 4 tsps butter
- 1/4 C. brown sugar
- 1 C. non-dairy creamer
- 4 tbsps milk
- 1/4 C. brown sugar

Directions

- Cook your oats in boiling water for 6 mins.
- Get the bowl that you will use for serving and add in 1 tbsp of butter and sugar to each. Then add your preferred amount of oatmeal.
- Top your oatmeal with another tbsp of milk and brown sugar, and one fourth a C. of creamer.
- Enjoy immediately.

Amount per serving (4 total)

Timing Information:

Preparation	Cooking	Total Time
5 m	10 m	15 m

Nutritional Information:

Calories	347 kcal
Fat	13 g
Carbohydrates	52.7g
Protein	6.5 g
Cholesterol	12 mg
Sodium	187 mg

* Percent Daily Values are based on a 2,000 calorie diet.

EASY SOUTH AMERICAN STYLE OATS

Ingredients

- 1 1/2 C. milk
- 1/2 C. quick cooking oats
- 2 tbsps white sugar
- 1/4 tsp ground cinnamon
- 1 pinch ground nutmeg
- 1 pinch salt

Directions

- For 4 min simply boil all the ingredients. Enjoy warm.

Amount per serving (2 total)

Timing Information:

Preparation	Cooking	Total Time
10 m	5 m	15 m

Nutritional Information:

Calories	220 kcal
Fat	5.1 g
Carbohydrates	35.2g
Protein	8.7 g
Cholesterol	15 mg
Sodium	270 mg

* Percent Daily Values are based on a 2,000 calorie diet.

OVEN OATS II

Ingredients

- 1/2 C. vegetable oil
- 3/4 C. white sugar
- 2 eggs
- 1 C. milk
- 1/2 tsp salt
- 1 tbsp baking powder
- 3 C. quick cooking oats
- 1/2 C. raisins
- 2 tbsps brown sugar
- 1/2 tsp ground cinnamon

Directions

- Combine the following evenly: oatmeal, oil, baking powder, sugar, salt, raisins, milks, and eggs.
- Enter everything into a casserole dish coated with nonstick spray then garnish with some cinnamon and brown sugar.
- Let the contents chill in the fridge for 8 hours then cook in the oven for 40 mins at 350 degrees.
- Enjoy.

Amount per serving (8 total)

Timing Information:

Preparation	Cooking	Total Time
10 m	35 m	45 m

Nutritional Information:

Calories	378 kcal
Fat	17.8 g
Carbohydrates	49.8g
Protein	6.7 g
Cholesterol	49 mg
Sodium	305 mg

* Percent Daily Values are based on a 2,000 calorie diet.

CROCK POT OATS II

Ingredients

- 1 C. oats
- 3 C. water
- 1 pinch salt
- 1 C. half-and-half cream
- 1/4 C. brown sugar, or to taste

Directions

- For 6 to 8 hours cook your oats in water on low in the crock pot.
- Then add in your half and half and salt when it has fully cooked.
- Garnish your bowl of oatmeal with some brown sugar.

Amount per serving (4 total)

Timing Information:

Preparation	Cooking	Total Time
2 m	8 h	8 h 2 m

Nutritional Information:

Calories	208 kcal
Fat	8.3 g
Carbohydrates	29.8g
Protein	4.5 g
Cholesterol	22 mg
Sodium	35 mg

* Percent Daily Values are based on a 2,000 calorie diet.

ALMOND AND OATS

Ingredients

- 1 (1 oz.) packet instant oatmeal, unsweetened
- 1/2 C. hot milk or water
- 1 tbsp almond butter
- 1 red apple, cored and roughly chopped
- 1/4 C. whole natural almonds
- 1/2 tsp cinnamon
- 2 tsps honey

Directions

- Heat your milk in the microwave or a small saucepan.
- Put your oatmeal in the same bowl that you will eat out of. Then cover it with the milk and almond butter.
- Add in your almonds, honey, apples, and cinnamon.
- Enjoy.

Amount per serving (1 total)

Timing Information:

Preparation	Cooking	Total Time
5 m		10 m

Nutritional Information:

Calories	594 kcal
Fat	31.9 g
Carbohydrates	67.6g
Protein	18 g
Cholesterol	10 mg
Sodium	198 mg

* Percent Daily Values are based on a 2,000 calorie diet.

PUMPKIN, PECAN, AND OATS

Ingredients

- 2 C. steel cut oats
- 2 C. diced apple
- 1 C. dried cranberries
- 1/2 C. slivered almonds
- 1/2 C. chopped pecans
- 3 C. water
- 1 C. milk
- 1 tbsp ground cinnamon
- 1 tsp pumpkin pie spice
- 2 tsps butter

Directions

- Cook all the ingredients for 8 hours with low heat. Enjoy warm in the morning.

Amount per serving (8 total)

Timing Information:

Preparation	Cooking	Total Time
10 m	8 h	8 h 10 m

Nutritional Information:

Calories	326 kcal
Fat	12.5 g
Carbohydrates	48.2g
Protein	8.2 g
Cholesterol	5 mg
Sodium	24 mg

* Percent Daily Values are based on a 2,000 calorie diet.

ROLLED OATS AND BANANA

Ingredients

- 1 C. uncooked rolled oats
- 1 C. whole wheat flour
- 3/4 C. all-purpose flour
- 1/4 C. brown sugar
- 2 tbsps dry milk powder
- 2 tsps baking powder
- 1/2 tsp baking soda

- 1/2 tsp salt
- 1 egg
- 2 C. milk
- 2 tbsps vegetable oil
- 1 tsp vanilla extract
- 1 banana, mashed

Directions

- Blend your oats until powdery.
- Sift or mix the follow in a bowl: baking soda and powder, oats, salt, regular flour and wheat flour, milk powder, and brown sugar. Place everything to the side.
- Get a 2nd bowl, mix: beaten eggs, mashed banana, vanilla, and veggie oil.
- Combine both bowls and let the contents sit for 10 mins.
- Grease a frying pan and then heat it.
- Cook large spoonfuls of the mix for about 2 mins per side. Continue for all ingredients.
- Enjoy with maple syrup.

Amount per serving (6 total)

Timing Information:

Preparation	Cooking	Total Time
15 m	15 m	30 m

Nutritional Information:

Calories	333 kcal
Fat	8.5 g
Carbohydrates	54.7g
Protein	11 g
Cholesterol	38 mg
Sodium	524 mg

* Percent Daily Values are based on a 2,000 calorie diet.

Maggie's Favorite Porridge

Ingredients

- 3 C. water
- 1 C. powdered milk
- 1 1/2 C. rolled oats
- 1/2 tsp ground cinnamon
- 1/2 C. raisins

- 1/2 tsp vanilla extract
- 3 eggs
- 4 tsps butter
- 1 C. milk
- 3 tbsps honey

Directions

- Get some water boiling then combine in your cinnamon, powdered milk, and oats. Once boiling again lower the heat and let the contents simmer for 12 mins.
- Shut off the heat and add in your vanilla and raisins.
- One by one add your eggs and make sure to stir them in completely.
- Enter your porridge into a bowl and garnish each with some honey, 1 tsp of butter, and one fourth C. of milk.
- Enjoy.

Amount per serving (4 total)

Timing Information:

Preparation	Cooking	Total Time
5 m	10 m	20 m

Nutritional Information:

Calories	507 kcal
Fat	20.5 g
Carbohydrates	64.2g
Protein	19.2 g
Cholesterol	151 mg
Sodium	237 mg

* Percent Daily Values are based on a 2,000 calorie diet.

EGG AND AVOCADO ROLLED OATS

Ingredients

- 1 1/2 C. So Delicious(R) Dairy Free Original Culinary Coconut Milk
- 1 1/2 C. water
- 1 1/2 tsps sea salt
- 1/2 C. rolled oats
- 1/2 C. steel cut oats
- 1 hardboiled egg, chopped
- half avocado, sliced

Directions

- Boil your milk and water in a big pan then add your salt, steel cut and rolled oats. Once boiling set the heat to low then let the oats lightly boil for 21 mins.
- Before serving add your chopped hard boiled eggs, and avocados. Enjoy warm.

Amount per serving (2 total)

Timing Information:

Preparation	Cooking	Total Time
10 m	30 m	40 m

Nutritional Information:

Calories	542 kcal
Fat	35.3 g
Carbohydrates	52g
Protein	9.9 g
Cholesterol	0 mg
Sodium	1349 mg

* Percent Daily Values are based on a 2,000 calorie diet.

OATS AND PEACH

Ingredients

- 1/2 (15 oz.) can sliced peaches, drained
- 1/2 C. water
- 1/2 C. milk
- 1/2 C. quick-cooking oats
- 2 tbsps packed brown sugar
- 1/4 tsp ground cinnamon, or more to taste
- 1 pinch salt

Directions

- Get a bowl and mix: peaches, cinnamon, water, salt, brown sugar, oats, and milk.
- Cook contents in the microwave for 4 mins.
- Halfway through the cooking time stop the microwave and stir the contents.
- If oats get too thick add a tbsp of water and continue microwaving.
- Enjoy.

Amount per serving (1 total)

Timing Information:

Preparation	Cooking	Total Time
5 m	3 m	8 m

Nutritional Information:

Calories	411 kcal
Fat	5.1 g
Carbohydrates	84.5g
Protein	10.7 g
Cholesterol	10 mg
Sodium	460 mg

* Percent Daily Values are based on a 2,000 calorie diet.

Quinoa and Banana

Ingredients

- 1/4 C. water
- 1/4 C. skim milk
- 1 tbsp quinoa
- 1/2 small banana, sliced
- 1 1/2 tbsps rolled oats
- 1 tbsp oat bran
- 1 pinch salt
- 1 pinch ground cinnamon
- 1 tbsp chopped walnuts
- 1 tsp brown sugar
- 1/4 tsp vanilla extract

Directions

- Boil: quinoa, milk, and water. Once boiling lower the heat and lightly boil for 6 mins.
- Add your salt, cinnamon, banana, oat bran, and rolled oats.
- Stir for 6 mins until everything achieves your desired level of thickness.
- Turn off the heat and add your vanilla, walnuts, and brown sugar.
- Enjoy.

Amount per serving (1 total)

Timing Information:

Preparation	Cooking	Total Time
5 m	15 m	20 m

Nutritional Information:

Calories	220 kcal
Fat	6.6 g
Carbohydrates	37g
Protein	7.3 g
Cholesterol	1 mg
Sodium	418 mg

* Percent Daily Values are based on a 2,000 calorie diet.

STEEL OATS AND APPLE

Ingredients

- cooking spray
- 8 C. water
- 23 oz. unsweetened applesauce
- 1 1/2 C. steel cut oats
- 2 Granny Smith apples - peeled, cored, and diced
- 1/4 C. ground cinnamon, or to taste
- 1/3 C. granular no-calorie sweetener

Directions

- Coat your slow cooker with non-stick spray. Then add: sweetener, water, cinnamon, applesauce, diced apple, and oats.
- Cook everything on low for about 6 hours.
- Enjoy.

Amount per serving (10 total)

Timing Information:

Preparation	Cooking	Total Time
15 m	6 h	6 h 15 m

Nutritional Information:

Calories	140 kcal
Fat	1.6 g
Carbohydrates	29.9g
Protein	3.3 g
Cholesterol	0 mg
Sodium	8 mg

* Percent Daily Values are based on a 2,000 calorie diet.

Cocoa Wet Oats

Ingredients

- 2 C. boiling water
- 1 C. rolled oats
- 1/4 tsp salt
- 1/2 C. brown sugar
- 1 banana, mashed
- 1/4 C. semisweet chocolate chips

Directions

- For 6 mins boil your oats in salted water. Turn off the heat and place a lid on the pot. Let the contents sit for about 4 more mins to get thick.
- Add your chocolate, bananas, and sugar before serving and stir the contents.
- Enjoy.

Amount per serving (2 total)

Timing Information:

Preparation	Cooking	Total Time
10 m	5 m	15 m

Nutritional Information:

Calories	516 kcal
Fat	9.1 g
Carbohydrates	108.1g
Protein	6.9 g
Cholesterol	0 mg
Sodium	319 mg

* Percent Daily Values are based on a 2,000 calorie diet.

ROLLED OATS AND ALMOND MILK

Ingredients

- 2 C. rolled oats
- 3 1/2 C. sweetened vanilla almond milk
- 1/8 tsp salt
- 1/2 C. dried tart cherries

Directions

- Microwave all the ingredients except the cherries for 4 mins.
- Stir the contents at 2 mins.
- Before serving the oatmeal add in your cherries.
- Enjoy.

Amount per serving (4 total)

Timing Information:

Preparation	Cooking	Total Time
5 m	5 m	10 m

Nutritional Information:

Calories	266 kcal
Fat	4.9 g
Carbohydrates	53.1g
Protein	6.5 g
Cholesterol	< 1 mg
Sodium	206 mg

* Percent Daily Values are based on a 2,000 calorie diet.

OVERNIGHT OATS I

Ingredients

- 1/3 C. milk
- 1/4 C. rolled oats
- 1/4 C. Greek yogurt
- 2 tsps chia seeds
- 2 tsps honey
- 1 tsp ground cinnamon
- 1/4 C. fresh blueberries

Directions

- Get a jar and add into it: cinnamon, milk, honey, oats, chia seeds, and yogurt. Place a lid on the jar and shake the contents for 1 to 2 mins.
- Add in your blueberries and shake again.
- Let the jar sit in the fridge for at least 7 hrs.
- Enjoy on the go.

Amount per serving (1 total)

Timing Information:

Preparation	Cooking	Total Time
5 m		8 h 5 m

Nutritional Information:

Calories	279 kcal
Fat	9.6 g
Carbohydrates	41.1g
Protein	9.5 g
Cholesterol	18 mg
Sodium	69 mg

* Percent Daily Values are based on a 2,000 calorie diet.

Overnight Oats II

Ingredients

- 1/2 C. old-fashioned oats
- 1/2 C. Greek yogurt
- 1/2 C. unsweetened almond milk
- 1/2 C. diced peaches
- 1 packet stevia powder
- 1 tsp chia seeds (optional)
- 1/2 tsp ground cinnamon, or more to taste
- 1/2 tsp almond extract
- 2 tbsps chopped pecans, or to taste (optional)

Directions

- Get a jar and add in: cinnamon, oats, almond extract, yogurt, chia seeds, almond milk, stevia, and peaches.
- Place a lid on the jar and shake the contents for 1 to 2 mins.
- Add in your pecans and shake again.
- Place the contents in the fridge for at least 7 hrs.
- Enjoy.

Amount per serving (1 total)

Timing Information:

Preparation	Cooking	Total Time
15 m		8 h 15 m

Nutritional Information:

Calories	455 kcal
Fat	25.4 g
Carbohydrates	44.6g
Protein	13.7 g
Cholesterol	22 mg
Sodium	151 mg

* Percent Daily Values are based on a 2,000 calorie diet.

CARDAMOM AND ROSE

Ingredients

- 1/2 C. steel-cut oats
- 2 C. So Delicious(R) Dairy Free Unsweetened Coconut Milk
- 1 small pear, chopped
- 1/2 tsp vanilla extract
- 1/2 tsp rose water
- 1/2 tsp almond extract
- 1/4 tsp cardamom
- 1/4 tsp cinnamon
- Sweetener of choice, to taste

Directions

- Coat your slow cooker with some nonstick spray then add everything listed besides the sweetener to the slow cooker.
- For 8 hrs let the contents cook on low.
- After 8 hrs has elapsed add your sweeteners.
- Enjoy.

Amount per serving (4 total)

Timing Information:

Preparation	Cooking	Total Time
5 m	7 h	7 h 5 m

Nutritional Information:

Calories	125 kcal
Fat	3.8 g
Carbohydrates	19.9g
Protein	3.2 g
Cholesterol	0 mg
Sodium	8 mg

* Percent Daily Values are based on a 2,000 calorie diet.

CHAPTER 2: WAFFLE RECIPES

WAFFLE I (VANILLA)

Ingredients

- 2 C. all-purpose flour
- 1 tsp salt
- 4 tsps baking powder
- 2 tbsps white sugar
- 2 eggs
- 1 1/2 C. warm milk
- 1/3 C. butter, melted
- 1 tsp vanilla extract

Directions

- Get a bowl, mix: sugar, flour, baking powder, and some salt.
- Get your waffle iron heated.
- Get a 2nd bowl, mix: whisked eggs, vanilla, butter, and milk.
- Combine both bowls. Evenly mix them. Pour mixture over the waffle iron. Heat until golden.
- Plate and eat warm.
- Enjoy.

Servings: 10 to 12 waffles

Nutrition

Timing Information:

Preparation	Cooking	Total Time
10 mins	15 mins	25 mins

Nutritional Information:

Calories	379 kcal
Carbohydrates	47.6 g
Cholesterol	113 mg
Fat	16.2 g
Fiber	1.4 g
Protein	10.2 g
Sodium	899 mg

* Percent Daily Values are based on a 2,000 calorie diet.

YEAST WAFFLE

Ingredients

- 2 C. milk
- 1 package yeast
- 1/2 C. warm water
- 1/2 C. butter, melted
- 1 tsp salt
- 1 tsp white sugar
- 3 C. flour
- 2 eggs, whisked
- 1/2 tsp baking soda

Directions

- Get a saucepan and heat the milk until simmering. Then set it aside.
- Get a bowl add some yeast, warm water, and mix them evenly. Let it sit for 12 mins.
- Get a 2nd bowl, mix: flour, milk, sugar, yeast mix, salt, and butter. Make a batter with a mixer. Put a lid on the bowl and let it rest overnight.
- When ready combine in some baking soda and whisked eggs, mix evenly.
- Use nonstick spray on your waffle iron. Then ladle your batter into it. Heat until cooked fully.
- Enjoy warm.

Servings: 6 to 8 servings

Timing Information:

Preparation	Cooking	Total Time
30 mins	10 mins	14 hrs

Nutritional Information:

Calories	434 kcal
Carbohydrates	52.8 g
Cholesterol	109 mg
Fat	19.3 g
Fiber	1.9 g
Protein	11.8 g
Sodium	660 mg

* Percent Daily Values are based on a 2,000 calorie diet.

Waffle Sandwich I
(Fried Chicken Tenders)

Ingredients

- 4 eggs
- 1/4 C. heavy cream
- 2 tbsps cayenne pepper
- 1 tbsp salt
- 1 tbsp ground black pepper
- 2 C. all-purpose flour
- 1 C. cornstarch
- 1 tbsp salt
- 1 quart peanut oil for frying

- 8 chicken tenders
- 1 C. mayonnaise
- 1/4 C. maple syrup
- 2 tsps prepared horseradish
- 1 tsp dry mustard powder
- 12 slices bacon
- 8 thin slices Cheddar cheese
- 8 plain frozen waffles

Directions

- Get a bowl, mix: black pepper, beaten eggs, 1 tbsp of salt, cayenne, and cream.
- Get a 2nd bowl, sift in evenly: 1 tbsp salt, cornstarch, and flour.
- Coat your chicken, first dip it into the eggs, then into the flour mix. Set chicken to the side for 25 mins.
- Get a deep fryer. Heat your oil.

- With a batch process: fry chicken pieces for 9 mins each or until crisp and fully done. Remove excess oils. Set aside.
- Get a 3rd bowl, mix: mustard powder, mayo, horse-radish, and maple syrup.
- Get a frying pan and fry your bacon until crisp or for 12 mins.
- Preheat your broiler, to low if possible.
- Lay out 4 waffles on a broiler safe dish. On each waffle put: 2 chicken tenders, 2 pieces of cheddar, and 3 bacon strips.
- Melt the cheese with your broiler. Top each waffle with other waffles. But first add mayo to each.
- Enjoy.

Servings: 4 sandwiches

Timing Information:

Preparation	Cooking	Total Time
15 mins	30 mins	1 hr 5 mins

Nutritional Information:

Calories	1793 kcal
Carbohydrates	127.1 g
Cholesterol	397 mg
Fat	109.9 g
Fiber	4.8 g
Protein	72.9 g
Sodium	5234 mg

* Percent Daily Values are based on a 2,000 calorie diet.

A WAFFLE FROM BELGIUM

Ingredients

- 1 package active dry yeast
- 1/4 C. warm milk
- 3 egg yolks
- 2 3/4 C. warm milk
- 3/4 C. butter, melted and cooled
- 1/2 C. white sugar
- 1 1/2 tsps salt
- 2 tsps vanilla extract
- 4 C. all-purpose flour
- 3 egg whites

Directions

- Get a bowl, mix: one fourth C. of room temp. milk, and yeast. Set aside for 12 mins until it becomes creamy.
- Get a 2nd bowl, mix: one fourth C. room temp milk, beaten eggs, and melted butter.
- Combine both bowls. Then add: vanilla, salt, and sugar. Add the rest of the flour and milk (2.5 C.).
- Whisk egg whites vigorously. Combine with batter. Place a lid on everything. Let it stand for 1.5 hours.
- Get your waffle iron hot. Coat with nonstick spray. Cook .5 C. of batter until golden.
- Enjoy warm.

Servings: 8 waffles

Timing Information:

Preparation	Cooking	Total Time
15 mins	20 mins	1 hr 35 mins

Nutritional Information:

Calories	506 kcal
Carbohydrates	65.3 g
Cholesterol	130 mg
Fat	21.4 g
Fiber	1.9 g
Protein	12.3 g
Sodium	622 mg

* Percent Daily Values are based on a 2,000 calorie diet.

WAFFLE II (VANILLA)

Ingredients

- 2 eggs
- 2 C. all-purpose flour
- 1 3/4 C. milk
- 1/2 C. vegetable oil
- 1 tbsp white sugar
- 4 tsps baking powder
- 1/4 tsp salt
- 1/2 tsp vanilla extract

Directions

- Get your waffle iron hot.
- Get a bowl, mix evenly: whisk eggs, veggie oil, vanilla, flour, salt, milk, baking powder, and sugar.
- Coat your iron with nonstick spray. Ladle batter onto the iron. Cook until golden enjoy.

Servings: 6 servings

Timing Information:

Preparation	Cooking	Total Time
5 mins	15 mins	20 mins

Nutritional Information:

Calories	382 kcal
Carbohydrates	38 g
Cholesterol	68 mg
Fat	21.6 g
Fiber	1.1 g
Protein	8.7 g
Sodium	390 mg

* Percent Daily Values are based on a 2,000 calorie diet.

EASY BUTTERMILK WAFFLE

Ingredients

- 2 1/4 C. flour
- 1 tsp baking soda
- 1 tsp baking powder
- 1/2 tsp salt
- 1/4 C. butter
- 1/4 C. brown sugar
- 3 egg yolks
- 2 C. buttermilk
- 3 egg whites

Directions

- Get your waffle iron hot.
- Get a bowl, mix evenly: salt, flour, baking powder and soda.
- Get a 2nd bowl, mix: brown sugar, whisked eggs, cream butter, buttermilk.
- Combine bowl 1 and 2 to form a batter.
- Get a 3rd bowl: Beat egg whites until stiff (an upward motion from the whisk produces a peak).
- Mix in 1/3 of your eggs into the batter until smooth. Then add the rest. Continue mixing until completely smooth.
- Coat your iron with nonstick spray. Ladle batter onto the iron. Cook until crispy.
- Enjoy warm.

Servings: 6 waffles

Timing Information:

Preparation	Cooking	Total Time
15 mins	5 mins	45 mins

Nutritional Information:

Calories	329 kcal
Carbohydrates	46.2 g
Cholesterol	126 mg
Fat	11.1 g
Fiber	1.3 g
Protein	10.8 g
Sodium	638 mg

* Percent Daily Values are based on a 2,000 calorie diet.

Waffle III

(Potatoes)

Ingredients

- 2 tbsps butter
- 1 onion, chopped
- 1 tbsp minced garlic
- 2 C. mashed potatoes
- 1/4 C. all-purpose flour
- 2 eggs
- 1/4 tsp salt
- 1/4 tsp ground black pepper

Directions

- Get a frying pan. Heat it up. Then melt your butter. Stir fry garlic and onions for 8 mins.
- Get your waffle iron hot.
- Get a bowl, evenly mix: black pepper, fried garlic and onions, salt, mashed potatoes, eggs, flour, and salt.
- Coat your iron with nonstick spray.
- With a batch process cook 1/3 C. of batter on the iron until crispy (4 mins usually). continue for all batter.
- Enjoy warm.

Servings: 4 servings

Timing Information:

Preparation	Cooking	Total Time
10 mins	15 mins	25 mins

Nutritional Information:

Calories	217 kcal
Carbohydrates	27.9 g
Cholesterol	110 mg
Fat	9 g
Fiber	2.3 g
Protein	6.5 g
Sodium	540 mg

* Percent Daily Values are based on a 2,000 calorie diet.

HEALTHIER WHEAT APPLESAUCE WAFFLE

Ingredients

- cooking spray
- 8 eggs, beaten
- 7 C. water
- 1 C. canola oil
- 1 C. unsweetened applesauce
- 4 tsps vanilla extract
- 4 C. whole wheat pastry flour
- 2 C. dry milk powder
- 2 C. flax seed meal
- 1 C. wheat germ
- 1 C. all-purpose flour
- 1/4 C. baking powder
- 4 tsps baking powder
- 1/4 C. white sugar
- 1 tbsp ground cinnamon
- 1 tsp salt

Directions

- Get your waffle iron hot.
- Get a bowl, evenly mix: vanilla extract, whisked eggs, applesauce, canola oil, and water.
- Get a 2nd bowl, sift: salt, wheat pastry flour, cinnamon, dry milk powder, 1/4 C. and 4 tsps of baking powder, flax seed meal, general flour, and wheat germ.
- Combine both bowls.
- Coat your iron with nonstick spray.
- With a batch process: cook 1/2 a C. of batter until crispy. Continue for all batter.
- Enjoy.

Servings: 24 servings

Timing Information:

Preparation	Cooking	Total Time
10 mins	55 mins	1 hr 5 mins

Nutritional Information:

Calories	313 kcal
Carbohydrates	33.4 g
Cholesterol	64 mg
Fat	15.9 g
Fiber	6 g
Protein	11.8 g
Sodium	506 mg

* Percent Daily Values are based on a 2,000 calorie diet.

WAFFLE SANDWICH II (APPLES & SAUSAGE)

Ingredients

- 2 links pork sausage links
- 1 slice Cheddar cheese
- 2 frozen waffles, toasted
- 1/4 apple, sliced
- 1/2 tsp cinnamon-sugar

Directions

- Get a frying pan hot. Stir fry your sausages until fully cooked for 7 mins usually.
- Toast 1 waffle. Layer some cheddar cheese on it, and then apple slices. Garnish with sugar and cinnamon. Add a final layer of sausage and add another waffle to form a sandwich.
- Cut into two pieces. Enjoy

Servings: 1 waffle sandwich

Timing Information:

Preparation	Cooking	Total Time
5 mins	5 mins	10 mins

Nutritional Information:

Calories	469 kcal
Carbohydrates	37.3 g
Cholesterol	80 mg
Fat	26.6 g
Fiber	2.4 g
Protein	20 g
Sodium	907 mg

* Percent Daily Values are based on a 2,000 calorie diet.

WAFFLE IV (GINGER)

Ingredients

- 1 tbsp butter, softened
- 2 tbsps molasses
- 1/4 C. liquid egg substitute
- 1/2 C. Kamut flour
- 1/2 C. whole wheat pastry flour
- 1 tsp baking powder
- 1/4 tsp baking soda
- 1/8 tsp sea salt
- 1 tsp ground ginger
- 1/2 tsp cinnamon
- 1/8 tsp ground cloves
- 3/4 C. boiling water, or as needed

Directions

- Get a bowl, mix evenly: egg substitute, butter, and molasses.
- Get a 2nd bowl, sift: cloves, whole wheat flour, cinnamon, baking soda and powder, ginger, and salt.
- Combine both bowls with some water and flour. Mix until even.
- Heat your waffle iron. Cover with nonstick spray.
- Ladle batter onto the iron. Cook until crispy. Continue with remaining batter.
- Enjoy.

Servings: 4 servings

Timing Information:

Preparation	Cooking	Total Time
20 mins	10 mins	30 mins

Nutritional Information:

Calories	177 kcal
Carbohydrates	29.7 g
Cholesterol	8 mg
Fat	4.1 g
Fiber	3.4 g
Protein	6 g
Sodium	308 mg

* Percent Daily Values are based on a 2,000 calorie diet.

CORNMEAL WAFFLE

Ingredients

- 1 C. all-purpose flour
- 1 C. stone-ground cornmeal
- 2 tsps baking powder
- 1 tsp baking soda
- 1/2 tsp salt
- 1/3 C. vegetable oil
- 2 eggs
- 2 C. buttermilk
- 1 tbsp oil, or as needed for greasing

Directions

- Get a bowl, sift: salt, flour, baking soda and soda.
- Get a 2nd bowl, mix evenly: buttermilk, veggie oil (1/3 C.), and beaten eggs.
- Combine both bowls evenly to make batter.
- Heat waffle iron and coat with nonstick spray.
- Ladle enough batter to fill 75% of the iron's surface. Cook until golden. Repeat for all batter.
- Enjoy.

Servings: 5 waffles

Timing Information:

Preparation	Cooking	Total Time
10 mins	5 mins	15 mins

Nutritional Information:

Calories	415 kcal
Carbohydrates	46.3 g
Cholesterol	78 mg
Fat	21 g
Fiber	1.8 g
Protein	10.3 g
Sodium	813 mg

* Percent Daily Values are based on a 2,000 calorie diet.

Mediterranean Waffle (Garbanzo Beans)

Ingredients

- nonstick spray
- 2 (15 oz) cans garbanzo beans (chickpeas), drained and rinsed
- 1 medium onion, chopped
- 2 large egg whites
- 1/4 C. chopped fresh cilantro
- 1/4 C. chopped fresh parsley
- 3 cloves roasted garlic, or more to taste
- 1 1/2 tbsps all-purpose flour
- 2 tsps ground cumin
- 1 3/4 tsps salt
- 1 tsp ground coriander
- 1/4 tsp ground black pepper
- 1/4 tsp cayenne pepper
- 1 pinch ground cardamom

Directions

- Heat your waffle cooker.
- Process the following with your food processor: cardamom, garbanzo beans, cayenne, egg whites, black pepper, cilantro, coriander, parsley, salt, cumin, and flour, and garlic
- Process until you have a smooth mixture. Enter everything into a bowl.
- Coat your iron with nonstick spray. For 6 mins cook 1/4 C. of mixture. Continue with remaining mixture. Enjoy warm.

Servings: 4 servings

Timing Information:

Preparation	Cooking	Total Time
15 mins	15 mins	30 mins

Nutritional Information:

Calories	210 kcal
Carbohydrates	38.7 g
Cholesterol	0 mg
Fat	2.1 g
Fiber	7.5 g
Protein	10 g
Sodium	1471 mg

* Percent Daily Values are based on a 2,000 calorie diet.

Cottage Cheese Cinnamon Waffle

Ingredients

- 1 C. old-fashioned oats
- 1 C. cottage cheese
- 2 eggs
- 3 egg whites
- 1 tsp honey
- 1 splash pure vanilla extract
- 1 pinch ground cinnamon

Directions

- Heat your waffle cooker.
- Get your blender, blend until smooth: cinnamon, oats, vanilla extract, egg whites, cottage cheese, and eggs
- With a batch process: cook batter for 5 mins. Continue for remaining.
- Enjoy.

Servings: 3 waffles

Timing Information:

Preparation	Cooking	Total Time
10 mins	5 mins	15 mins

Nutritional Information:

Calories	254 kcal
Carbohydrates	23.2 g
Cholesterol	135 mg
Fat	8.5 g
Fiber	2.9 g
Protein	20.8 g
Sodium	408 mg

* Percent Daily Values are based on a 2,000 calorie diet.

Chicken Nugget Waffle

Ingredients

- 24 frozen chicken nuggets
- cooking spray
- 1 1/4 C. all-purpose flour
- 1/4 C. cornmeal
- 1 1/2 tsps white sugar
- 1 1/2 tsps baking powder
- 1 tsp salt
- 3/4 tsp baking soda
- 1/2 tsp ground black pepper
- 1/4 tsp cayenne pepper
- 1 3/4 C. buttermilk
- 1/3 C. vegetable oil
- 2 eggs, beaten

Directions

- Set your oven to 400 degrees before doing anything else.
- Cook your chicken nuggets for 15 mins. Until golden.
- Heat your waffle cooker.
- Get a bowl, sift evenly: Cayenne pepper, flour, black pepper, sugar, baking soda and salt.
- Get a 2nd bowl, mix: eggs, buttermilk, and oil.
- Combine both bowls to make batter. Evenly mix everything.
- Coat your iron with nonstick spray.
- In the middle of your iron put a piece of chicken. Take a tbsp of batter and coat the nugget. Cook for 5 mins. Repeat with all nuggets.
- Enjoy warm.

Servings: 6 servings

Timing Information:

Preparation	Cooking	Total Time
15 mins	25 mins	40 mins

Nutritional Information:

Calories	489 kcal
Carbohydrates	40.6 g
Cholesterol	109 mg
Fat	27.5 g
Fiber	1.3 g
Protein	19.7 g
Sodium	1155 mg

* Percent Daily Values are based on a 2,000 calorie diet.

Coconut Waffle

Ingredients

- 2 C. spelt flour
- 1/4 C. flax seed meal
- 4 tsps baking powder
- 1 tbsp ground cinnamon
- 2 tsps baking soda
- 1 tsp Himalayan salt
- 1 3/4 C. coconut milk
- 1/4 C. coconut oil, melted
- 2 eggs, beaten
- 2 tbsps apple cider vinegar
- 1 tbsp vanilla extract

Directions

- Get your waffle cooker hot.
- Get a bowl, sift: salt, spelt flour, baking soda and powder, flax seed meal, and cinnamon.
- Get a 2nd bowl, mix evenly: vanilla extract, coconut milk, vinegar, eggs, and coconut oil.
- Mix both bowls evenly for make batter. Let it sit for 5 mins.
- Coat your iron with nonstick spray.
- Cook for 7 mins 1 C. of batter.
- Enjoy warm.

Servings: 8 waffles

Timing Information:

Preparation	Cooking	Total Time
15 mins	30 mins	45 mins

Nutritional Information:

Calories	303 kcal
Carbohydrates	25.1 g
Cholesterol	46 mg
Fat	20.8 g
Fiber	3 g
Protein	7.2 g
Sodium	805 mg

* Percent Daily Values are based on a 2,000 calorie diet.

Buttermilk Greek Waffle

Ingredients

- 2 1/2 C. all-purpose flour
- 4 tsps baking powder
- 3/4 tsp salt
- 2 C. buttermilk
- 1/2 C. vanilla Greek-style yogurt
- 1/2 C. butter, melted
- 2 eggs, beaten
- 1 1/2 tbsps white sugar
- 3/4 C. chopped strawberries

Directions

- Get your waffle maker hot.
- Get a bowl, sift: salt, flour, and baking powder.
- Get a 2nd bowl, evenly mix: sugar, buttermilk, eggs, Greek yogurt, butter, and strawberries.
- Mix both bowls to make batter.
- Coat waffle iron with nonstick spray. For 8 mins cook 1/3 C. of batter. Cook all the batter in this manner.
- Enjoy.

Servings: 6 servings

Timing Information:

Preparation	Cooking	Total Time
15 mins	20 mins	35 mins

Nutritional Information:

Calories	414 kcal
Carbohydrates	49.8 g
Cholesterol	107 mg
Fat	18.9 g
Fiber	1.8 g
Protein	11.5 g
Sodium	839 mg

* Percent Daily Values are based on a 2,000 calorie diet.

Autumn Waffle

(Pumpkin, Molasses)

Ingredients

- 1 C. all-purpose flour
- 1 tsp baking powder
- 1/2 tsp baking soda
- 1/4 tsp salt
- 3/4 tsp ground cinnamon
- 1/2 tsp ground ginger
- 1/8 tsp ground nutmeg
- 2 tsps canola oil
- 1 tsp molasses
- 1/4 C. canned pumpkin
- 1 C. buttermilk
- 1 large egg
- 2 tbsps sugar or Splenda
- 1 1/2 C. maple syrup

Directions

- Get your waffle cooker hot.
- Get a bowl, sift: nutmeg, flour, ginger, baking soda and powder, cinnamon, and salt.
- Get a 2nd bowl, mix evenly: buttermilk, oil, pumpkin, and molasses.
- Get a 3rd bowl, combine: splenda, and beaten eggs.
- Mix all three bowls to form your batter.
- Coat your iron with nonstick spray. With a batch process cook: your batter until crispy. Continue for remaining. Enjoy warm.

Servings: 6 waffles

Timing Information:

Preparation	Cooking	Total Time
15 mins	5 mins	20 mins

Nutritional Information:

Calories	163 kcal
Carbohydrates	32.5 g
Cholesterol	33 mg
Fat	3 g
Fiber	1.2 g
Protein	4.8 g
Sodium	418 mg

* Percent Daily Values are based on a 2,000 calorie diet.

WAFFLE V

(VEGAN APPROVED)

Ingredients

- 6 tbsps water
- 2 tbsps flax seed meal
- 1 C. rolled oats
- 1 3/4 C. soy milk
- 1/2 C. all-purpose flour
- 1/2 C. whole wheat flour
- 2 tbsps canola oil
- 4 tsps baking powder
- 1 tsp vanilla extract
- 1 tbsp agave nectar
- 1/2 tsp salt

Directions

- Get your waffle maker hot.
- With your blender process your oats.
- Get a bowl, mix: flax meal and water.
- Add to your blender the following: salt, flour, agave nectar, wheat flour, vanilla extract, canola, and baking powder. Blend until batter like.
- Add nonstick spray to iron.
- Cook 1/2 C. of batter until crispy. Repeat.
- Enjoy.

Servings: 6 waffles

Timing Information:

Preparation	Cooking	Total Time
10 mins	30 mins	40 mins

Nutritional Information:

Calories	229 kcal
Carbohydrates	33.1 g
Cholesterol	0 mg
Fat	8.1 g
Fiber	4.1 g
Protein	7 g
Sodium	558 mg

* Percent Daily Values are based on a 2,000 calorie diet.

Waffle VI

(Chocolate)

Ingredients

- 2 1/4 C. all-purpose flour
- 1/2 C. white sugar
- 1 tbsp baking powder
- 3/4 tsp salt
- 3/4 C. butter
- 1 C. chocolate chips
- 1 1/2 C. milk
- 6 egg whites
- 1 tbsp vanilla extract

Directions

- Get a bowl, sift: salt, flour, baking powder, and sugar.
- In a 2nd bowl, microwave for 1.5 mins: chocolate chips and butter. Stop and mix the contents together. Microwave for another 45 secs. Do this until completely smooth. Remove and let cool.
- Get your waffle iron hot.
- Once no longer hot, mix the following with the chocolate: vanilla, milk, and egg whites.
- Coat your iron with nonstick spray.
- Cook batter until crispy. Continue for all batter.
- Enjoy warm.

Servings: 10 waffles

Timing Information:

Preparation	Cooking	Total Time
10 mins	10 mins	20 mins

Nutritional Information:

Calories	376 kcal
Carbohydrates	44.4 g
Cholesterol	40 mg
Fat	19.8 g
Fiber	1.8 g
Protein	7.1 g
Sodium	424 mg

* Percent Daily Values are based on a 2,000 calorie diet.

A Waffle from Norway

Ingredients

- 2 eggs
- 2 tbsps white sugar
- 3 tbsps melted shortening
- 1 3/4 C. milk
- 1 tsp salt
- 1 tsp vanilla extract
- 1 1/2 C. all-purpose flour
- 3 1/2 tsps baking powder

Directions

- Get your waffle maker hot.
- Get a bowl, combine until stiff: sugar and eggs with a mixer.
- Add to the same bowl: vanilla, shortening, salt, and milk.
- Now you want use your sifter to add baking soda and flour and continue mixing.
- Add nonstick spray to your batter.
- Cook 2/3 C. of batter until golden. Continue for remaining batter.
- Enjoy.

Servings: 4 servings

Timing Information:

Preparation	Cooking	Total Time
10 mins	20 mins	30 mins

Nutritional Information:

Calories	373 kcal
Carbohydrates	48.2 g
Cholesterol	102 mg
Fat	14.6 g
Fiber	1.3 g
Protein	11.5 g
Sodium	976 mg

* Percent Daily Values are based on a 2,000 calorie diet.

WAFFLE VII

(BANANA)

Ingredients

- 1 1/4 C. all-purpose flour
- 3 tsps baking powder
- 1/2 tsp salt
- 1 pinch ground nutmeg

- 1 C. 1% milk
- 1 egg
- 2 ripe bananas, sliced

Directions

- Get your waffle maker hot.
- Get a bowl, sift: nutmeg, flour, salt, and baking powder.
- Get a 2nd bowl, mix evenly: whisked eggs, and milk.
- Combine both bowls to make batter.
- Cover iron with nonstick spray.
- In the middle of your iron put 2.5 tbsps of batter. Then layer bananas. Then another 2 tbsps.
- Cook until golden. Repeat for all batter.
- Enjoy.

Servings: 4 servings

Timing Information:

Preparation	Cooking	Total Time
10 mins	30 mins	45 mins

Nutritional Information:

Calories	241 kcal
Carbohydrates	47.3 g
Cholesterol	50 mg
Fat	2.5 g
Fiber	2.6 g
Protein	8.3 g
Sodium	606 mg

* Percent Daily Values are based on a 2,000 calorie diet.

Waffle VIII

(Cinnamon)

Ingredients

- 2 C. all-purpose flour
- 1/4 C. white sugar
- 1/2 C. brown sugar
- 2 1/2 tsps ground cinnamon
- 4 tsps baking powder
- 1/4 tsp salt

- 1 3/4 C. milk
- 1/2 C. vegetable oil
- 1 tsp vanilla extract
- 2 egg whites
- nonstick spray

Directions

- Get a bowl, sift evenly: baking powder, sugar, salt, cinnamon, and brown sugar.
- Get a 2nd bowl, mix: vanilla extract, milk, and veggie oil.
- Combine both bowls to form batter.
- Get a 3rd bowl and beat egg whites until the eggs form peaks when lifting the whisk straight up.
- Add eggs to batter evenly.
- Get your iron hot and coated with nonstick spray.
- With a batch process cook: batter until none remains. Enjoy.

Servings: 18 small square waffles

Timing Information:

Preparation	Cooking	Total Time
15 mins	15 mins	30 mins

Nutritional Information:

Calories	154 kcal
Carbohydrates	21.1 g
Cholesterol	2 mg
Fat	6.7 g
Fiber	0.5 g
Protein	2.6 g
Sodium	159 mg

* Percent Daily Values are based on a 2,000 calorie diet.

A Waffle from Scandinavia

Ingredients

- 2 eggs, separated
- 1/4 C. white sugar
- 1 tsp vanilla sugar
- 1/4 C. water
- 3 tbsps butter, melted
- 1 C. buttermilk
- 1 1/2 C. all-purpose flour
- 1/4 tsp ground cardamom
- 1 pinch salt

Directions

- Get a bowl, mix: sugar and eggs until slightly froth-like.
- Combine until smooth: water, vanilla, melted butter, sugar, flour, and buttermilk.
- Get a 2nd bowl, mix: eggs until stiff. Then mix with batter until smooth.
- Get your iron and coated with nonstick spray.
- Cook 1/3 C. of batter for 6 mins. Repeat for remaining batter.
- Enjoy.

Servings: 5 waffles

Timing Information:

Preparation	Cooking	Total Time
20 mins	20 mins	40 mins

Nutritional Information:

Calories	288 kcal
Carbohydrates	42 g
Cholesterol	95 mg
Fat	9.7 g
Fiber	1 g
Protein	8.1 g
Sodium	130 mg

* Percent Daily Values are based on a 2,000 calorie diet.

A Waffle from Denmark
(Sweet Potato)

Ingredients

- 4 C. all-purpose flour
- 1 C. white sugar
- 4 tsps baking powder
- 4 tsps baking soda
- 9 eggs, separated
- 1 1/2 C. buttermilk
- 1 1/2 C. milk
- 3 tbsps vanilla extract
- 1/4 C. butter, melted

Directions

- Get a bowl, sift: baking soda and powder, sugar, and flour.
- Get a 2nd bowl, mix until smooth: butter, egg yolks, milk, and buttermilk.
- Get a 3rd bowl: whisk egg whites until soft peaks form.
- Combine all the bowls, until smooth.
- Heat your iron and coat it with nonstick spray.
- Cook half a C. of batter until golden. Repeat for remaining batter.
- Enjoy.

Servings: 14 waffles

Timing Information:

Preparation	Cooking	Total Time
15 mins	15 mins	30 mins

Nutritional Information:

Calories	293 kcal
Carbohydrates	45 g
Cholesterol	131 mg
Fat	7.6 g
Fiber	1 g
Protein	9.5 g
Sodium	606 mg

* Percent Daily Values are based on a 2,000 calorie diet.

Sweet Potato Waffle II

Ingredients

- 1 C. canned sweet potato puree
- 3 egg yolks
- 1 C. milk
- 1 1/2 C. cake flour
- 1 tbsp baking powder
- 1 tbsp white sugar
- 1 tsp salt
- 1 tsp ground nutmeg
- 1/4 C. chopped pecans
- 3 egg whites
- 3 tbsps butter, melted
- 2 tbsps pecans, chopped

Directions

- Heat your waffle maker.
- Get a bowl, mix: 1/4 C. pecans, flour, nutmeg, sugar, baking powder, and salt.
- Get a 2nd bowl, mix: milk, sweet potato puree, and yolk.
- Combine both bowls to form a batter.
- Get a 3 bowl to mix your egg whites until peaks form. Add egg whites and melted butter to your batter mix until everything is smooth.
- Coat waffle iron with nonstick spray.
- Cook batter until golden. Top with pecans after finished.

Servings: 6 waffles

Timing Information:

Preparation	Cooking	Total Time
20 mins	20 mins	40 mins

Nutritional Information:

Calories	338 kcal
Carbohydrates	44 g
Cholesterol	121 mg
Fat	14.4 g
Fiber	2.1 g
Protein	9 g
Sodium	753 mg

* Percent Daily Values are based on a 2,000 calorie diet.

Veggie Oat Waffle

(Zucchini, Oatmeal)

Ingredients

- 1 1/2 C. milk
- 1 C. shredded zucchini
- 2 eggs
- 2 tbsps butter, melted
- 1 1/2 C. whole wheat flour

- 1 C. quick-cooking oats
- 1 tbsp baking powder
- 2 tbsps brown sugar
- 1 tsp salt
- 1 tsp ground cinnamon

Directions

- Get your iron hot.
- Get a bowl, mix: butter, milk, eggs, and zucchini.
- Get a 2nd bowl, sift: cinnamon, flour, salt, oats, brown sugar, and baking powder.
- Combine both bowls, slowly and evenly until smooth.
- Add a ladle full of batter to your iron and cook for 6 mins.
- Repeat for all batter.
- Enjoy warm.

Servings: 8 waffles

Timing Information:

Preparation	Cooking	Total Time
15 mins	30 mins	45 mins

Nutritional Information:

Calories	198 kcal
Carbohydrates	29.8 g
Cholesterol	58 mg
Fat	6.1 g
Fiber	4.1 g
Protein	7.7 g
Sodium	478 mg

* Percent Daily Values are based on a 2,000 calorie diet.

CHAPTER 3: EGG RECIPES

EGGS IN BREAD

Ingredients

- 1/2 tbsp butter
- 1 slice white bread
- 1 egg

Directions

- Coat your bread with butter on each of its sides. Then cut-out a circle in the middle of it.
- Whisk your egg in a small bowl. Set it aside.
- Get a skillet hot and for 1 min fry each side of the bread. Pour the egg into the hole and cook for 3 more mins.
- Enjoy.

Amount per serving (1 total)

Timing Information:

Preparation	Cooking	Total Time
10 m	10 m	20 m

Nutritional Information:

Calories	189 kcal
Fat	11.6 g
Carbohydrates	13g
Protein	8.3 g
Cholesterol	201 mg
Sodium	281 mg

* Percent Daily Values are based on a 2,000 calorie diet.

Parmesan Zucchini Eggs

Ingredients

- 4 eggs, lightly beaten
- 2 tbsps grated Parmesan cheese
- 2 tbsps olive oil
- 1 zucchini, sliced 1/8- to 1/4-inch thick
- garlic powder, or to taste
- salt and ground black pepper to taste

Directions

- Get a bowl, evenly mix: parmesan and whisked eggs.
- Get a 2nd small bowl, combine in: pepper, garlic powder, and salt.
- Fry your zucchini in olive oil for 8 mins. Pour in the seasonings from the 2nd bowl. Lower the heat and then pour in the first bowl.
- Cook eggs for 4 mins. Turn off the heat and place a lid on the pan for 2 mins until the eggs are completely done.

Amount per serving (4 total)

Timing Information:

Preparation	Cooking	Total Time
10 m	15 m	25 m

Nutritional Information:

Calories	147 kcal
Fat	12.5 g
Carbohydrates	1.6g
Protein	7.6 g
Cholesterol	188 mg
Sodium	111 mg

* Percent Daily Values are based on a 2,000 calorie diet.

FRIED SAUSAGE AND EGGS

Ingredients

- 1 lb pork sausage meat
- 2 tsps Worcestershire sauce
- 4 hard-cooked eggs, peeled
- 1 tbsp all-purpose flour
- 1/8 tsp salt
- 1/8 tsp ground black pepper
- 1 egg, whisked
- 2/3 cup dry bread crumbs
- 1 quart oil for deep frying

Directions

- Get a bowl, evenly mix: Worcestershire, pepper, sausage, salt and flour. Split the mix into four parts.
- Wrap each of the four eggs with an equal part of sausage mix.
- Get 2 bowls. Put whisked eggs into one bowl. Crumbled bread into another bowl. Coat each wrapped egg first with whisked eggs then dip into the bread.
- Get some oil hot to 365 degrees in a large skillet, saucepan, or fryer and cook the eggs in the oil for 6 mins.

Amount per serving (4 total)

Timing Information:

Preparation	Cooking	Total Time
20 m	10 m	30 m

Nutritional Information:

Calories	659 kcal
Fat	53.9 g
Carbohydrates	16.5g
Protein	25.9 g
Cholesterol	323 mg
Sodium	1324 mg

* Percent Daily Values are based on a 2,000 calorie diet.

TOMATO FETA EGGS

Ingredients

- 1 tbsp butter
- 1/4 cup chopped onion
- 4 eggs, beaten
- 1/4 cup chopped tomatoes
- 2 tbsps crumbled feta cheese
- salt and pepper to taste

Directions

- Fry onions until see-through, in butter, in a frying pan. Then mix in your eggs. While the eggs are frying make sure to stir them so that they become scrambled.
- Before the eggs are completely cooked add in your pepper and salt, then your feta, and finally your tomatoes.
- Continue to let the eggs fry until the feta melts.

Amount per serving (4 total)

Timing Information:

Preparation	Cooking	Total Time
10 m	5 m	15 m

Nutritional Information:

Calories	116 kcal
Fat	8.9 g
Carbohydrates	2g
Protein	7.2 g
Cholesterol	198 mg
Sodium	435 mg

* Percent Daily Values are based on a 2,000 calorie diet.

EGGS FROM FRANCE

Ingredients

- 1/2 cup butter
- 1/2 cup flour
- salt and pepper to taste
- 1 quart milk

- 8 slices white bread, toasted
- 8 hard-cooked eggs
- 1 pinch paprika

Directions

- First get a saucepan hot before doing anything else.
- Enter your butter into the saucepan and let it melt completely.
- Then add in your flour, stir it a bit, and let it cook for 10 mins until it becomes lighter in colour.
- Mix in your milk and wait until everything is lightly boiling, then set the heat to low.
- Let it cook for 10 more mins.
- Add in some pepper and salt.
- Remove the yolks from each egg. Then you want to dice the egg whites and mix them into the simmering sauce.
- Get a strainer and press the eggs through it. Put this in a bowl.
- Put half a cup of simmering sauce on a piece of toasted bread and garnish the bread with the yolks and some paprika.
- Enjoy.

Amount per serving (8 total)

Timing Information:

Preparation	Cooking	Total Time
10 m	20 m	30 m

Nutritional Information:

Calories	336 kcal
Fat	20.1 g
Carbohydrates	25g
Protein	13.2 g
Cholesterol	252 mg
Sodium	413 mg

* Percent Daily Values are based on a 2,000 calorie diet.

Romano and Pepperoni Eggs

Ingredients

- 1 cup egg substitute
- 1 egg
- 3 green onions, thinly sliced
- 8 pepperoni slices, diced
- 1/2 tsp garlic powder
- 1 tsp melted butter
- 1/4 cup grated Romano cheese
- 1 pinch salt and ground black pepper to taste

Directions

- Get a bowl, evenly mix the following in order: garlic powder, egg substitute, pepperoni, green onions, and egg.
- Fry your eggs in melted butter in a covered frying pan with low heat for 14 mins.
- Before serving garnish with Romano cheese and pepper and salt.
- Enjoy.

Amount per serving (2 total)

Timing Information:

Preparation	Cooking	Total Time
10 m	10 m	20 m

Nutritional Information:

Calories	266 kcal
Fat	16.2 g
Carbohydrates	3.7g
Protein	25.3 g
Cholesterol	124 mg
Sodium	586 mg

* Percent Daily Values are based on a 2,000 calorie diet.

MACARONI AND EGGS

Ingredients

- 1 1/2 cups elbow macaroni
- 1 tbsp butter
- 1/4 tsp paprika (optional)
- salt and ground black pepper to taste
- 4 large eggs, lightly beaten

Directions

- Boil macaroni in salt and water for 9 mins until al dente.
- Get a frying pan and melt some butter in it. Then add in your pasta to the melted butter along with some: pepper, paprika, and salt.
- Add eggs to the pasta and do not stir anything for 2 mins. Then for 6 mins continue cooking the eggs but now you can stir. Turn off the heat.
- Place a lid on the pan and let the eggs continue to cook without heat.

Amount per serving (4 total)

Timing Information:

Preparation	Cooking	Total Time
10 m	15 m	25 m

Nutritional Information:

Calories	243 kcal
Fat	8.5 g
Carbohydrates	29.9g
Protein	11.5 g
Cholesterol	194 mg
Sodium	93 mg

* Percent Daily Values are based on a 2,000 calorie diet.

Florentine Style

Ingredients

- 2 tbsps butter
- 1/2 cup mushrooms, sliced
- 2 cloves garlic, minced
- 1/2 (10 oz.) package fresh spinach
- 6 large eggs, slightly beaten
- salt and ground black pepper to taste
- 3 tbsps cream cheese, cut into small pieces

Directions

- Fry your garlic and mushrooms in melted butter in a frying pan for 2 mins. Then mix in your spinach and cook this for another 4 mins.
- Finally add some pepper and salt and your eggs to the mix and let the eggs set completely. Once the eggs have set you want to flip them.
- Add a bit of cream cheese to the eggs and let it cook for about 4 mins.

Amount per serving (3 total)

Timing Information:

Preparation	Cooking	Total Time
10 m	10 m	20 m

Nutritional Information:

Calories	279 kcal
Fat	22.9 g
Carbohydrates	4.1g
Protein	15.7 g
Cholesterol	408 mg
Sodium	276 mg

* Percent Daily Values are based on a 2,000 calorie diet.

Scrambled Eggs Done Right

Ingredients

- 3 large eggs
- 1 pinch red pepper flakes
- 9 cherry tomatoes, halved
- 2 tbsps crumbled feta cheese
- 1 tbsp very thinly sliced fresh basil leaves
- olive oil
- 1 pinch sea salt

Directions

- Get a bowl and evenly mix the following: basil, eggs, feta, red pepper flakes, and tomatoes.
- Fry in hot olive oil for a few secs without any stirring so the eggs set. Then begin to scramble them for 1 min.
- Ideally you want your eggs to be only lightly set. Remove them from the heat. Season with salt.
- Enjoy.

Amount per serving (1 total)

Timing Information:

Preparation	Cooking	Total Time
5 m	5 m	10 m

Nutritional Information:

Calories	420 kcal
Fat	33.1 g
Carbohydrates	9.7g
Protein	23.1 g
Cholesterol	575 mg
Sodium	755 mg

* Percent Daily Values are based on a 2,000 calorie diet.

CHIPOTLE BACON AND EGGS

Ingredients

- 4 slices bacon, chopped
- 6 eggs
- 2 tbsps sour cream
- 1 tbsp oil, or as needed
- 1 tbsp chipotle-flavored hot sauce (such as Tabasco(R) Chipotle Pepper Sauce)
- 3 vine-ripened tomatoes, chopped
- 1 avocado - peeled, pitted, and chopped
- 1 (6 oz.) package fresh spinach
- 1/2 cup shredded Cheddar cheese
- salt and ground black pepper to taste

Directions

- Get a bowl, evenly mix: sour cream and eggs.
- Fry your bacon for 11 mins. Then remove oil excess with some paper towels.
- Now you want to cook your eggs in oil in a frying pan for 7 minutes with your hot sauce.
- Add in your spinach, avocadoes and tomatoes and cook for 1 more min.
- Finally top everything with cheddar and a bit more pepper and salt. Let the cheese melt with another .5 to 1 min of cooking time.

Amount per serving (4 total)

Timing Information:

Preparation	Cooking	Total Time
10 m	20 m	30 m

Nutritional Information:

Calories	381 kcal
Fat	29.6 g
Carbohydrates	12.2g
Protein	20.5 g
Cholesterol	310 mg
Sodium	553 mg

* Percent Daily Values are based on a 2,000 calorie diet.

Breakfast Eggs from India

Ingredients

- 1/4 cup vegetable oil
- 1 tsp garam masala
- 1 tsp ground turmeric
- 1 tsp ground coriander
- salt to taste
- 1/2 cup finely chopped onion
- 3 green chili peppers, sliced
- 2 large eggs

Directions

- Get a bowl and add your eggs to it. Then whisk them.
- In a frying pan, cook the following in hot oil for 6 mins: salt, green chili peppers, garam masala, onions, coriander, and turmeric.
- After 6 mins pour in your eggs to the seasoned onions and chilies and scramble for 5 mins.

Amount per serving (2 total)

Timing Information:

Preparation	Cooking	Total Time
5 m	10 m	15 m

Nutritional Information:

Calories	367 kcal
Fat	32.9 g
Carbohydrates	12.4g
Protein	8.4 g
Cholesterol	186 mg
Sodium	157 mg

* Percent Daily Values are based on a 2,000 calorie diet.

Fried Eggs and Shrimp

Ingredients

- 1 tbsp vegetable oil, or as needed
- 1 onion, chopped
- 6 eggs, beaten
- 1 tsp salt
- 10 cooked large shrimp
- 1/4 cup cocktail sauce

Directions

- Fry onions in hot oil for 11 mins. Then mix in the eggs and salt. Continue frying for 6 mins.
- Add in your shrimp and cocktail sauce and continue to cook for 5 more mins.
- Enjoy.

Amount per serving (3 total)

Timing Information:

Preparation	Cooking	Total Time
10 m	15 m	25 m

Nutritional Information:

Calories	236 kcal
Fat	14.9 g
Carbohydrates	8.8g
Protein	16.8 g
Cholesterol	404 mg
Sodium	1237 mg

* Percent Daily Values are based on a 2,000 calorie diet.

Maggie's Favorite Eggs

Ingredients

- 1 (1 lb) bulk pork sausage
- 12 eggs, beaten
- 1/3 cup sour cream
- 1 (7 oz.) can chopped green chilies
- 1 (24 oz.) jar salsa
- 1 cup shredded Cheddar cheese
- 1 cup shredded Monterey Jack cheese
- 1/2 cup pickled jalapeno pepper slices, or to taste
- 2 avocados, sliced

Directions

- Coat a baking dish with oil or nonstick spray and set your oven to 350 degrees before doing anything else.
- Get a bowl and whisk all your eggs together in it. Enter the eggs into the greased dish. And bake it in the oven for 15 mins.
- For 8 mins fry your sausage in hot oil and then crumble.
- After eggs have baked for 15 mins remove them from the oven layer your sausage, jalapeno, salsa, green chilies, Monterey, and cheddar over the eggs.
- Put everything back in the oven for 23 mins.
- Enjoy. With a topping of avocado.

Amount per serving (8 total)

Timing Information:

Preparation	Cooking	Total Time
15 m	40 m	55 m

Nutritional Information:

Calories	492 kcal
Fat	38.2 g
Carbohydrates	12.8g
Protein	27 g
Cholesterol	343 mg
Sodium	1683 mg

* Percent Daily Values are based on a 2,000 calorie diet.

EASY SPICY EGGS

Ingredients

- 2 hard-cooked eggs, cut in half lengthwise
- 1 tbsp cream-style horseradish sauce

Directions

- Take your eggs and take out the yolks. Put the yolks aside in a bowl.
- Add horseradish to the yolks and mix everything evenly.
- Simply fill each egg white with the yolk mix and chill before serving them.

Amount per serving (4 total)

Timing Information:

Preparation	Cooking	Total Time
10 m		10 m

Nutritional Information:

Calories	46 kcal
Fat	3.4 g
Carbohydrates	0.4g
Protein	3.3 g
Cholesterol	108 mg
Sodium	33 mg

* Percent Daily Values are based on a 2,000 calorie diet.

Buttery Eggs

Ingredients

- 6 eggs
- 2 tbsps butter
- 2 tbsps all-purpose flour
- 2 cups milk
- 1/8 tsp ground white pepper, if desired
- salt and pepper to taste

Directions

- Get a big saucepan and fill it with water. Add your eggs to the water and bring it to a rolling boil. Once boiling for about a minute then remove the pan from the heat and place a lid on it. Let it stand for about 13 mins.
- After 13 mins take out the eggs, remove the shells, and dice them.
- Now drain the saucepan of its water and melt some butter in it. Once the butter is melted add some flour and heat it until a ball-like shape begins to form. Then add in your milk and lightly stir until the sauce begins to boil.
- While boiling add in: salt, white pepper, chopped eggs, and black pepper. Heat everything up then remove it all from the heat.
- Enjoy with your favorite toasted bread.

Amount per serving (3 total)

Timing Information:

Preparation	Cooking	Total Time
10 m	10 m	20 m

Nutritional Information:

Calories	311 kcal
Fat	20.9 g
Carbohydrates	12.4g
Protein	18.6 g
Cholesterol	405 mg
Sodium	261 mg

* Percent Daily Values are based on a 2,000 calorie diet.

Breakfast In Texas

Ingredients

- 1 lb sausage
- 9 slices white bread, cut into cubes
- 9 eggs, beaten
- 1 (11 oz.) can condensed cream of Cheddar cheese soup
- 3 cups milk
- 1 1/2 tsps salt
- 8 oz. shredded Cheddar cheese

Directions

- Before doing anything else grease a baking dish some butter.
- Get a frying pan and stir fry your sausage and then crumble it. Cook until it is fully done. Remove oil excess.
- Get a bowl combine evenly: salt, eggs, milk, and soup.
- Enter into your baking dish the cubed bread, and sausage.
- Pour the wet mix over the bread cubes in the baking dish. Then top everything with cheese.
- Cover the dish with foil and put it in the frig throughout the night.
- Once 8 hours has elapsed you want to set the oven to 350 degrees. Once the oven is hot bake the casserole for at least an hour.
- Enjoy.

Amount per serving (6 total)

Timing Information:

Preparation	Cooking	Total Time
30 m	25 m	55 m

Nutritional Information:

Calories	799 kcal
Fat	58.3 g
Carbohydrates	30.8g
Protein	36.8 g
Cholesterol	392 mg
Sodium	2120 mg

* Percent Daily Values are based on a 2,000 calorie diet.

Eggs from Ireland

Ingredients

- 2 tbsps butter
- 6 potatoes, peeled and sliced
- 1 onion, minced
- 1 green bell pepper, chopped
- 6 eggs, beaten

Directions

- In hot oil and in a frying pan cook your onions, potatoes, and peppers until the potatoes are fully browned.
- Simple add your eggs to the potatoes and continue frying until the eggs are firm.
- Enjoy.

Amount per serving (4 total)

Timing Information:

Preparation	Cooking	Total Time
15 m	20 m	35 m

Nutritional Information:

Calories	425 kcal
Fat	13.6 g
Carbohydrates	62.6g
Protein	15.1 g
Cholesterol	294 mg
Sodium	297 mg

* Percent Daily Values are based on a 2,000 calorie diet.

Eggs from Mexico

Ingredients

- 24 jalapeno peppers
- 1 lb sausage
- 2 cups all-purpose baking mix
- 1 (16 oz.) package Cheddar cheese, shredded
- 1 tbsp crushed red pepper flakes
- 1 tbsp garlic salt
- 1 (16 oz.) package Monterey Jack cheese, cubed

Directions

- Coat a casserole dish with nonstick spray and then set your oven to 325 degrees before doing anything else.
- Get a bowl, evenly mix: garlic salt, sausage, red pepper flakes, cheddar, and baking mix. Set aside.
- Take out the pulp and seeds in all the jalapenos by cutting an incision into each one and using your fingers to remove the insides.
- Fill the peppers with the Monterey cubes. Cover each pepper with the sausage mix in your bowl and try to shape everything into balls.
- Enter everything into the casserole dish and cook in the oven for 25 to 30 mins.
- Enjoy.

Amount per serving (12 total)

Timing Information:

Preparation	Cooking	Total Time
30 m	25 m	55 m

Nutritional Information:

Calories	541 kcal
Fat	42.3 g
Carbohydrates	15.7g
Protein	24.8 g
Cholesterol	98 mg
Sodium	1390 mg

* Percent Daily Values are based on a 2,000 calorie diet.

EGGS FROM ITALY

Ingredients

- 2 tbsps extra virgin olive oil
- 4 ripe tomatoes, chopped
- 4 eggs
- salt and pepper to taste

Directions

- For 6 mins cook your tomatoes in hot oil. Simply break the eggs into the tomatoes and add some pepper and salt. Fry until you reach the firmness that you enjoy the most.

Amount per serving (4 total)

Timing Information:

Preparation	Cooking	Total Time
5 m	10 m	15 m

Nutritional Information:

Calories	154 kcal
Fat	11.9 g
Carbohydrates	5.3g
Protein	7.5 g
Cholesterol	186 mg
Sodium	374 mg

* Percent Daily Values are based on a 2,000 calorie diet.

Vegetarian Eggs

Ingredients

- 1/4 cup olive oil
- 1/4 cup sliced fresh mushrooms
- 1/4 cup chopped onions
- 1/4 cup chopped green bell peppers
- 6 eggs
- 1/4 cup milk
- 1/4 cup chopped fresh tomato
- 1/4 cup shredded Cheddar cheese

Directions

- Get a bowl mix: milk, eggs, and veggies with tomatoes.
- Fry onions, mushrooms, and peppers until the onion are see-through in hot olive oil in a frying pan.
- Then pour in eggs and veggies continue cooking until the eggs are firm.
- Right before everything is finished top the eggs with your cheese and cook for another minute.
- Enjoy.

Amount per serving (6 total)

Timing Information:

Preparation	Cooking	Total Time
10 m	15 m	25 m

Nutritional Information:

Calories	182 kcal
Fat	15.8 g
Carbohydrates	2.4g
Protein	8.1 g
Cholesterol	192 mg
Sodium	159 mg

* Percent Daily Values are based on a 2,000 calorie diet.

Prosciutto Eggs

Ingredients

- 1 bunch fresh asparagus, trimmed
- 1 tbsp extra-virgin olive oil
- 1 tbsp olive oil
- 2 oz. minced prosciutto
- ground black pepper
- 1 tsp distilled white vinegar
- 1 pinch salt
- 4 eggs
- 1/2 lemon, zested and juiced
- 1 pinch ground black pepper

Directions

- Set your oven to 425 degree before doing anything else.
- Get a casserole dish and enter into it your asparagus and coat the veggies with some olive oil.
- Stir fry your prosciutto and some black pepper for 5 mins in 1 tbsp of olive oil.
- Layer the meat over the asparagus. Bake for 10 mins.
- Then toss the contents and bake for 6 more mins.
- Boil 3 inches of water and add in some salt and your vinegar.
- Then break an egg in the water. Continue for all eggs. Let the eggs poach for 6 mins. Then remove them from the water.
- Now plate your asparagus and coat them with a bit of lemon juice then topped with an egg. Then some zest of lemon and finally a bit of pepper.
- Enjoy.

Amount per serving (4 total)

Timing Information:

Preparation	Cooking	Total Time
15 m	25 m	40 m

Nutritional Information:

Calories	199 kcal
Fat	15.7 g
Carbohydrates	5.1g
Protein	10.8 g
Cholesterol	175 mg
Sodium	446 mg

* Percent Daily Values are based on a 2,000 calorie diet.

THANKS FOR READING! NOW LET'S TRY SOME **SUSHI** AND **DUMP DINNERS**....

http://bit.ly/2443TFg

To grab this **box set** simply follow the link mentioned above, or tap the book cover.

This will take you to a page where you can simply enter your email address and a PDF version of the **box set** will be emailed to you.

I hope you are ready for some serious cooking!

<u>http://bit.ly/2443TFg</u>

You will also receive updates about all my new books when they are free.

Also don't forget to like and subscribe on the social networks. I love meeting my readers. Links to all my profiles are below so please click and connect :)

<u>Facebook</u>

<u>Twitter</u>

Printed in Great Britain
by Amazon

37734844R00090